CRACKING YOUR BODY'S CODE

WORKBOOK

"Every health challenge presents the opportunity to transform a part of ourselves into something bigger and better."

-*Mauree Kai* FMCHC, BEP

Kai, Mauree, author

Published in the United States by Center for Holistic Healing Arts

www.MaureeKai.com

Title: Cracking Your Body's Code Workbook

Workbook—1st ed., October 2021

ISBN: 979-8-9850305-0-1

Introduction

As long as we are alive, we have the capacity to heal ourselves. We do not have to be victims to our present health challenges or genetics. With the right tools and support, many conditions can be reversed and resolved with diligence.

This workbook is designed to give you a variety of tools that you can apply to any situation with the intention of learning how to work with your symptoms to restore balance and transform your health if you stay consistent in your practices.

Each week a different topic will be presented with exercises to complete. They are designed to work with the physical, mental, emotional, and spiritual parts that make up who you are. It is important to create a clear vision in the very beginning of what healing you desire for yourself. You can do a section per week or take longer if you want to spend more time focusing on a particular exercise in the workbook.

It is my hope that this workbook will be a catalyst for a new healing paradigm that focuses on the whole person with the intention of supporting the body's innate healing ability; recognizing the connection between body, mind, and spirit; restoring health and well-being; and transforming lives in the process.

All the healing tools presented in this book were designed to empower you so you can create a healthier, more vibrant existence. It is your birthright to live a long and happy life. This workbook is not meant to replace traditional medicine or promote self-diagnosis. Rather, it is meant to give you the tools you need to facilitate true healing and start reclaiming your health. As long as you are alive, you have within you the power to restore your health and transform your life.

My wish is that you will feel empowered to take better control of your health and your life to become a better, healthier version of yourself!

Mauree Kai

ALSO BY MAUREE KAI

Cracking Your Body's Code – Keys to Transforming Symptoms into Message That Heal

The Language of Symptoms

"We explore the symptoms of suffering from the perspective that the malady itself is the pathway to awakening more fully to our true nature."

Robert Brumet

How wonderful is it that we can get up in the morning and have faith that our body knows just what to do to support us as we move through our daily activities! We get up, eat, and leave for work or school without giving the internal functions of our bodies much thought. We do not wonder if everything is going to function normally or if our bodies are going to stop us in our tracks. We often take for granted the overall health of our physical bodies and the many processes that go on to maintain our life on a daily basis—that is, until something hurts, or we don't feel quite right.

Our bodies have a built-in alarm system that notifies us when something is out of balance. We start to experience symptoms. Symptoms are meant to get our attention. They can be very subtle and almost undetectable at first. It is easier to notice sharp pains than it is to become aware of slight variations in how the body is feeling on a day to day basis. Oftentimes the smaller, minor symptoms are ignored, as we assume they are a passing anomaly and will go away as fast as they appeared. An occasional headache, bout of indigestion or diarrhea is dismissed as normal. Other times, symptoms are dismissed as being a normal occurrence because of age or family history. There is an existing belief structure that when you turn a certain age you are going to experience conditions like high blood pressure, elevated cholesterol, low energy, memory loss, or joint deterioration, and that it is a normal, expected part of the aging process. There is also a belief system that says we are victims of our genetics and will be in harm's way of some disease process because it "runs in the family." In the process of internalizing these beliefs we have allow our thoughts to resonate with them, accepting them as truth. When we do this, we are recreating the patterns through diet and lifestyle that activate those genes. Diabetes is a prime example.

The result is we manifest physical conditions that prove these beliefs to be true.

If a symptom lasts more than day, people habitually run to the pharmacy for an over-the-counter medicine to make the symptom go away. The symptom is considered an annoyance and the focus becomes, "How can I make it stop because it is interfering with my daily activities?" Antacids, aspirins, stool softeners, antihistamines, nasal decongestants, and sleep aids are just a few of the many common drugs sold like candy for the sole purpose of eliminating a symptom as quickly as it appeared. Then there are all the prescription drugs that are not only prescribed to eliminate a symptom but also to counteract reactions to other drugs! This has evolved out of a health care system that is really a disease management system.

What actually happens with a drug is that one set of symptoms is being exchanged for another set without knowing what caused the symptom in the first place. The focus is on eliminating the symptom with little or no consideration to what is happening in the whole person. You may suppress a symptom, but that doesn't resolve the underlying core issues. Every part of the body is connected to every other part in some manner. Emotions are intertwined with thoughts and the mind dwells within the body. Even a physical injury to a specific part of the body is going to have repercussions in another part of the body from the force of impact. While one part of the body may be exhibiting symptoms, it is not an isolated issue. Because everything in the body is connected and interdependent, other parts of the body are going to be affected in some manner by the symptoms you are experiencing.

Symptoms are created by the innate intelligence within our bodies to effectively communicate to our consciousness that something is out of balance and needs our attention. If the symptom goes unnoticed or unaddressed, it will eventually have a greater impact on our health and overall well-being by creating a ripple effect. You can suppress a symptom, but without the understanding of what caused it in the first place or what it is trying to communicate, nothing gets resolved and no permanent change will take place. The opportunity for deeper, lasting healing is then overlooked.

Symptoms are the universal language of our bodies.

Symptoms are the universal language of our physical bodies, presenting us with information we are not always conscious of in a manner we can understand. They orchestrate a dialogue between body, mind, and spirit. It is time we honored our physical bodies instead of suppressing them by paying attention to even the most subtle of symptoms and learning how to properly translate them into viable information that will lead us on a healing journey to greater vitality and well- being. The information conveyed within a symptom is as unique to the body as a fingerprint. While there are many conditions and imbalances that may present similar symptoms from person to person, the whole person needs to be taken into consideration to effectively translate the symptoms into information that is relevant and accurate to the individual. There is no one-size-fits-all with symptoms as each of us comes from a different background, different lifestyle, different belief system, and a different palate of personal challenges.

While we manifest a symptom on the physical level, the cause may very well originate on the mental, emotional, or even spiritual level. Because of the multi-dimensional aspect of our being, our physical bodies often reflect what is going on within other levels of our consciousness. By the time we have manifested a symptom, some form of stress has had an impact on our ability to internally maintain balance and alignment between body, mind, and spirit.

We are spiritual beings having a human experience. We may be limited in our understanding and awareness of our essence, but that is not sufficient reason to ignore who we really are and what we are capable of manifesting. To focus solely on the physical body during a healing process excludes other parts of our being that may be vital for true healing to occur. *The whole person* needs to be included in the evaluation of symptoms and the healing process that follows.

PERSONAL VISION

"As we think, so we create."

Write out your personal vision for optimal health and well-being in as much detail as possible. How do you want to feel, look, act, eat, and so forth. What type of relationships do you want to have? What do you see yourself doing with your life? What would make you the happiest?

____

____

____

____

____

____

____

____

____

____

____

____

____

____

____

____

____

____

For all those who have the desire to gain a deeper awareness of what true healing is
and want to empower themselves on their own personal healing journey.

Table of Contents

Week 1- *Quiet Please, Your Body is Talking*

"The greatest miracle on Earth is the human body. It is stronger than you may realize and improving its ability to self-heal is within your control."

Dr. Fabrizio Mancini

We are going to start with learning how to become aware of the subtle signals and symptoms coming from the body. Then, develop the ability to listen more closely and become aware of what the symptom or signal is trying to communicate to you.

Take a few moments to sit quietly and tune into our body. Just notice what you are feeling.

What area in your body is calling for attention?

Physical symptoms:

____

____

____

____

When did the symptoms start?

____

____

____

____

What was going on in your life at the time the symptoms first appeared?

____

____

____

____

What makes the symptoms feel worse?

____

____

____

____

What makes the symptoms feel better?

____

____

____

____

Does it have a color or a shape? Can you feel heat or cold coming from that part of your body?

____

____

____

____

If your symptoms could talk, what might they say to you?

____

____

____

____

Do any images or memories come to mind after focusing on this part of your body?

____

____

____

____

Do any actions steps come to mind that you could do? Maybe it is a dietary change or taking a walk. Perhaps you need to eliminate something or make a lifestyle change. Just be open to listening to what your body tells you *without judgment.* Write down your reflections here:

____

____

____

____

____

____

____

Make one new conscious choice/action a day that supports your vision for health and well-being.

Record your choices here:

MONDAY:

TUESDAY:

WEDNESDAY:

THURSDAY:

FRIDAY:

SATURDAY:

SUNDAY:

Week 2

Health and Healing: A Balancing Act

"Healing may not be so much about getting better, as about letting go of everything that isn't you – all of the expectations, all the beliefs, and becoming who you are."

Rachel Naomi Remen

We open the doorway to healing when we can view our suffering of a malady as a stepping stone rather than as a stumbling block. The path of healing is very personal and unique to the individual and yet there are obstacles to healing that are universal in nature. On a very basic level, there are common obstacles to healing such as toxicity in the body, poor diet, lack of exercise, chronic stress, holding onto negative emotions, and limiting core beliefs. If the physical body does not have the proper systemic support, the innate ability of the body to heal will be impeded. On the other hand, engaging in the proper healing modalities can activate the healing potential within as the body is self-correcting.

There are other obstacles that are just as vital but can be more elusive to the unaware person. The first obstacle I want to touch upon is the fear of change. It is human nature to want to stay within a comfort zone where we know what to expect, even if it is not serving us well, because change can be scary. Change means surrendering to the unknown and stepping more fully into personal power. Personal power is necessary to sustain health and wellness. Personal power is the mediator between our inner and outer worlds. An external concept of power without an internal sense of power leaves us open and vulnerable to health issues. There are images of power held in mass consciousness that equate power with money and control. True personal power comes from one's inner resources and innate intelligence and a belief in a higher power.

Another obstacle to healing is lack of self-care and self-love. To love yourself starts with accepting yourself just as you are in this moment. Instead of judging yourself harshly or placing unreasonable expectations upon yourself, to love yourself requires a willingness to appreciate, accept, support, and value who you are unconditionally in the here and now. Loving yourself means focusing on your strengths and being present with your feelings, whatever they are. Learn to see yourself as a unique, beautiful spiritual being who is fulfilling a purpose here on earth that no one else can do but you. You are the architect of your life given the power to create whatever you hold dear in your heart. You have been given the sole authority to decide what is right and true for you. Loving yourself means trusting your inner most knowing. This applies to you whether you are deciding what foods you want to put into your body, what activities bring you the most joy, what you most want to learn, or what healing path is right for you.

The third obstacle is the image we hold of ourselves in our minds. Our lives are shaped by our minds. The image we hold of ourselves will either promote our health and well-being or compromise it. When presented with a health challenge the worst thing you can do is let that challenge become part of your identity. People often say, "Well, my sister has this, and my mother had that so I guess I am bound to have it to." Another common phrase is, "It runs in the family." Then there is the most used phrase, I have……, as if taking full ownership of a health condition or disease process. There is a difference between saying "I am being challenged with" a particular condition and "I have" a particular condition. Words are very powerful. When we start a sentence with "I have" we are taking ownership and making it a part of our identity instead of expressing it in such a way that clearly states you are so much more than a health challenge you are dealing with. Look at are your predominant thoughts around a health condition. Whatever you are thinking and saying about it you may be manifesting more of the same. It is known that energy follows thought, no matter what the thought is. Energy doesn't discriminate between thoughts. So, we must discipline our thought processes that honor the Self and consciously create a healthy image of how we want to feel.

List the obstacles that are getting in the way of you feeling your best. They can be physical, mental, emotional, or spiritual. They can also be situations or conditions. Write them down without judgment of yourself.

____

____

____

____

____

____

____

Have any of these obstacles resulted from the lack of self-care? If so, which one(s)?

____

____

____

____

How can you improve upon your self-care?

____

____

____

____

____

Have any of these obstacles resulted from the lack of self-love?

____

____

____

____

____

What steps can you take to increase your self-love? Make a list here.

____

____

____

____

____

____

____

____

____

____

Consciously choose to take one action step every day that increases your self-care.

MONDAY:

TUESDAY:

WEDNESDAY:

THURSDAY:

FRIDAY:

SATURDAY:

SUNDAY:

Make one conscious choice every day to do something that is nurturing to yourself.

MONDAY:

TUESDAY:

WEDNESDAY:

THURSDAY:

FRIDAY:

SATURDAY:

SUNDAY:

At the end of your week, write down how your self-care choices went for you and how you feel now compared to the beginning of the week.

What do notice that is different from last week? How easy or difficult was it to take time to care for yourself?

____

____

____

____

____

____

____

____

____

____

____

____

____

____

____

____

____

____

____

____

Week 3

Food as Medicine

"Let food be thy medicine and medicine be thy food."

Hippocrates

Hippocrates, the father of Western medicine, placed high value on eating well and believed food had the potential to restore the body to good health. He is quoted as saying, "Let food be thy medicine and medicine be thy food." Thousands of years later, we are proving his theory to be true. Foods grown in the earth provide the nutritional components our bodies need and can also be used to support the body in a healing context. Add herbs and spices to that and you have access to nature's natural pharmacy. Our bodies know innately how to recover from injuries and heal wounds. Our bodies also know how to restore balance and produce energy. What is required from us is the right form of nourishment to support those internal processes. Poor food choices can be the cause of many adverse health conditions and conversely, healthy food choices can be the source of nutrients our bodies crave for healing.

Whether it is a raw diet, macrobiotics, vegan, vegetarian, grain free, gluten free, dairy free, Paleo, Keto, Pegan, or carbohydrate free, there are many documented case histories of people changing their diets and healing themselves of a health challenge.

There are certain foods that cause or contribute to a lot of health problems. They include but are not limited to: sugar, gluten, dairy, wheat, grains, trans fats, and preservatives. In addition, there are the top eight common allergens that cause issues for some people. They are: soy, eggs, milk, fish, wheat, shellfish, tree nuts, and peanuts. If you are having a lot of digestive distress, you may want to consider eliminating some of these foods for a week or two and see if your body and digestion feels better.

Write down what foods you are eliminating for at least a week. Record what changes you notice at the end of the week.

____

____

____

____

____

Think of the colors in the rainbow. Make a list of fruits and vegetables with each color. Add the colors to your daily plate that you are missing until you are eating a rainbow of colored wholesome food every day!

Red

____

Orange

____

Yellow

____

Green

____

Blue

____

Purple

____

____

PRIMARY FOODS

Primary foods are the things that make us feel alive and want to get up out of bed in the morning, greeting a new day with gratitude and joy for being alive. They can be grouped into four main categories: spirituality, career, relationships, and physical activity. Primary foods are what truly nourish us on a soul level. We are spiritual beings having a human experience. Our souls need to be fed from the living wellspring of life or our life force slowly drains out of us, eventually leaving us in a weakened and imbalanced state. If our souls are being fed with primary foods, chances are our physical bodies are going to respond favorably with energy, strength, and vitality. Then, the food we ingest is like icing on a cake!

Rank your level of satisfaction in each area of your life. The closer to 10 the more fulfilled you feel.

Once you have marked your number in each area, look at the lowest number areas. Pick one of those areas at a time and brainstorm ideas that would increase your level of satisfaction in that area.

Health and well-being   1   2   3   4   5   6   7   8   9   10

Home environment   1   2   3   4   5   6   7   8   9   10

Career   1   2   3   4   5   6   7   8   9   10

Fun and recreation   1   2   3   4   5   6   7   8   9   10

Significant/committed relationship   1   2   3   4   5   6   7   8   9   10

Friends   1   2   3   4   5   6   7   8   9   10

Family   1   2   3   4   5   6   7   8   9   10

Personal growth and development   1   2   3   4   5   6   7   8   9   10

Exercise   1   2   3   4   5   6   7   8   9   10

Week 4

Translating Symptoms into Messages

"Your biography becomes your biology."

Carolyn Myss

Identifying Symptoms

Symptoms are really a gift because they bring to your awareness a problem or issue within the body that was previously unknown to you. Symptoms, as I stated in an earlier chapter, are meant to get your attention. They are a very sophisticated form of communication from the intelligence within your body. Our natural impulse is to find a way to suppress or eliminate them without really understanding the root cause. If you suppress your symptoms, it is like putting your body on mute; as a result, you will disconnect yourself from your body's inner wisdom and miss the opportunity for healing your body is requesting.

The following applies to symptoms that have been nagging you or compromising your health in some manner. This information is to help you transform symptoms before you get to the point where you need medical intervention.

You want to spend time noticing what you notice. Take the time to quiet down your mind and sit with yourself. Without judgment, write down everything you feel, no matter how insignificant you may think it is. Also write down what parts of your body are involved.

Bring your focus into your physical body. Ask yourself the following questions:

- What physical symptoms do you notice?

- What part of the body is being affected?

- What makes the symptom worse?

- Do you feel it all the time or only at a certain time of the day or night?

- Do you feel better when you eat or when you don't eat?

- If your symptoms could talk, what would they say?

- How are the symptoms impacting your daily life?

After you have identified all the physical symptoms, you want to notice how you are feeling emotionally. Take an honest inventory of yourself:

·	Have you been feeling tense or anxious?

·	Are you sad or depressed?

·	How high is your stress level?

·	Do you wake up in the morning feeling optimistic and looking ahead to a brand new day or are you dragging yourself out of bed?

·	Do you find yourself getting caught up in the emotions of the drama on the news?

·	When did you first start noticing the symptoms?

·	What was going on in your life at that time?

In addition to your emotions, it is equally important to become aware of any limiting self-talk you have going on in your mind, or negative thinking in general. Since our mind exists within our bodies, the thoughts held in the mind are going to have a direct impact on the health of the body. Every cell in our body is enveloped with thought. Those thoughts have the power to heal or destroy. Are you thinking thoughts that build you up, make you feel strong, fill your heart with compassion and joy, or are you thinking thoughts that tell yourself you are limited in some way?

- Are you aware of limiting self-talk you habitually have going on in your mind?
- Do you have criticisms or judgments you find yourself saying over and over again?
- What thoughts or beliefs do you have about yourself that are not honoring and loving?

It has been proven that you can literally transform and rebuild the cells in your body by the power of your mind. So, it is important to know what you are thinking when you are experiencing symptoms. As you become aware of limiting thought patterns, you can replace them with more expanded thoughts that align with the truth of who you really are. Your mind can become your greatest ally in your healing process.

Exercise:

This week practice listening to your body and becoming more aware of all the subtle messages it is giving you. Take a 5-10 minutes each day and sit quietly and still your mental chatter. Reflect upon all the questions and then write down in detail your responses with as much detail as possible (without judgment). After you write out all your answers, notice the new awareness you received to your underlying health issues. You may need to do this a few days in a row until you get to the core issues. Be patient with yourself and as specific as possible.

Week 5 – From Suppression to Expression

"We explore the symptoms of suffering from the perspective that the malady itself is the pathway to awakening more fully to our true nature."

Robert Brumet

There may be a need to tend to the physical body first, depending on the circumstance, to keep the condition from spiraling out of control. When the physical body is presenting symptoms, it is bringing forth information about a condition that was previously unknown to the conscious mind. To only address the physical is to limit your innate ability to heal and live a more expanded version of yourself. Also, if you only address and treat the physical, you will be exchanging one set of symptoms for another without addressing the root cause.

At some point, suffering needs to be viewed from a higher perspective. It gives us the opportunity to deepen our understanding of our spiritual nature and learn how to work with spiritual law for true and lasting healing. Suffering can be our greatest teacher if we change our perception about how to manage it. We choose how we perceive the circumstances around suffering. No one else can dictate to us the thoughts and attitudes about our life. We alone determine what we will think and believe.

A great start for transforming suffering is to let go of any resistance you have and let suffering transform you. Let it be the key that opens the door into the deeper recesses of your mind where you can access your true nature that is healthy and whole. Hold steadfast to a vision of health and wholeness in your mind. Look for the gift or blessing within the conditions that you find yourself in. Above all, have compassion for yourself throughout your healing journey. Either suffering will master you or you will become the master over your suffering. You will transform your suffering when you are willing to take an honest inventory of your life and your beliefs about yourself and then raise your consciousness above your present conditions into a more expansive realm of thought where you can envision yourself healthy and whole.

Make a list of beliefs you have about yourself.

____

____

____

____

____

How do these beliefs limit you or impact your life?

____

____

____

____

____

____

____

"When you repress your emotions, you are working against them. When you express them harmfully, you're working for them. To experience them honorably means working with them, so they can heal and protect you as they were meant to."

Karla McLaren

Emotions are "energy in motion." They are a conscious mental reaction in response to circumstances, moods, and relationships with others. Emotions can represent a synthesis of personal experience, individual behaviors, and neuro-chemical activities that take place within the brain.

Over time we allow our thoughts to dictate who we believe we are and what we can and cannot do. These ideas can be our own creation or those of someone else, which we have accepted as true. Our feelings become the reflection of those thoughts and are expressed through our emotional nature. Our emotions are what give color to our personality and provide the fuel for authentic power.

Our role in maintaining our health is to become aware of what we are feeling and manage those feelings appropriately. If we neglect ourselves emotionally, we can become emotionally toxic which in turn has a negative impact on the health of our bodies. This toxic emotional energy gets stuck in the body causing distress in some part of the physical body. Many believe that toxic emotional stress levels are the origin of many diseases that ultimately manifest in the body. You may have heard the expression, "anger only hurts the person who is angry." We injure ourselves when we harbor negative emotions like anger, criticism, resentment, and even guilt. These emotions can and will be damaging over a period of time. Every emotion has a corresponding response system in the brain. In turn, they cause a physiological response in the body which is controlled by the sympathetic branch of the autonomic nervous system. You may experience these responses as a rapid heartbeat, restricted breathing, upset stomach, headaches, pain, elevated blood pressure, bowel disturbances, food cravings, and more, depending on your personal circumstance.

What "negative emotions do you struggle with? Anxiety, frustration, anger, grief, criticism, judgment, guilt, fear…?

____

____

____

____

____

Which of the emotions (anger, criticism, frustration, judgment, guilt, etc.) do you direct towards yourself or others? What does that look like?

____

____

____

____

____

How do these emotions affect your physical body? Do they cause you physical symptoms?

____

____

____

____

____

Identify the thoughts you have behind the emotions you have identified.

____

____

____

____

____

Pick one thought and reframe how you think about the situation or person? How can you see things differently? Can you take the thought and turn it into a more positive one that lifts you up?

____

____

____

____

____

Can you come up with one way the person or situation has helped you grow as a person? Every challenge has the potential to help you grow and evolve into a better version of yourself.

____

____

____

____

____

After deciding how you could see things differently, decide how you can express yourself in a more positive manner going forward. How can you respond in a more positive manner instead or reacting?

____

____

____

____

____

Notice how you feel differently in your body with a change in your perspective. Write down everything you notice.

Week 6

Tending the Mind's Garden

"If you want to see what your thoughts were yesterday, look at today. If you want to see what your body will look like tomorrow, look at your thoughts today."

Unknown

Core beliefs are formed in our minds based upon our perceptions of the world around us. They develop over time, not only from perceptions of our individual experiences, but also from other people's ways of thinking we take on as our own. Beliefs can be barriers or they can be bridges to something greater. They are not carved in stone, but rather exist as a structure in our own minds. We built them, and we can change them into something better if they are no longer serving our growth. Beliefs need to support our intentions for living healthy, fulfilling lives. They are influenced by daily experiences of security and safety, belonging and connectedness, love and appreciation, control and power, social and cultural roles, and sexuality. From this we formulate an image of ourselves, forming beliefs in our minds based upon our perceptions of the world around us. These beliefs are then reflected in our behavior, our appearance, and our health and well-being. To create any lasting kind of change in our health and well-being, we must become conscious of the thoughts that contributed to the condition in the first place and work to change them.

Core beliefs will fall into two categories: expansive and limiting. Expansive core beliefs always support our well-being and play a role in the evolution of our soul. They affirm the truth of who we are and help us to embrace the process of becoming even more. Some examples of expansive core beliefs might be statements such as "I am a unique and valuable person;" "I am the power and authority for what is best for me and my life;" "I am willing to grow through joy rather than suffering;" "It is safe for me to trust my intuition;" "I am worthy of experiencing greater health and vitality;" "I am strong and full of vitality;" "I am whole and complete;" or "I am confident and successful."

Limiting core beliefs, on the other hand, are rooted in misperceptions we have internalized about ourselves. In our minds, we may believe they are true, but in reality, they limit our ability to live healthy, vibrant lives. Examples of limiting core beliefs might be statements such as "I am not good enough;" "I am not worthy;" "No one loves me;" "I can't do anything right;" "No pain, no gain;" "I don't have a choice;" "I will never get better;" and "It is not safe to express myself."

Our bodies respond to our beliefs about love, value, image, and possibilities, regardless of the nature of the belief. To create lasting change in the health of our bodies, we need to become of aware of what is affecting it, the thoughts that are shaping it, and the beliefs that are limiting it. One of the greatest challenges in changing a limiting core belief is to not get distracted by what is going on around you or what others may be telling you. Your truth always comes from within and will make you feel better about yourself: more alive, more vital, more hopeful, and more empowered. When you speak truthful words about yourself, the cells in your body respond by aligning with the energy of those words and resonating with them. Within the words of truth are seeds of transformation. In transforming limited beliefs held in your mind, you will stimulate the life force that can heal your body. As we think, so we create.

Identify and write down limiting core beliefs you know you have about yourself.

____

____

____

____

____

____

____

____

Take time to be still and create expansive core beliefs for yourself to replace the limiting ones you identified. Then notice what you feel in your body when you think or say the words.

When you speak truthful words about yourself, the cells in your body respond by aligning with the positive energy of those words and resonating with them. Within the words of truth are seeds of transformation.

By transforming limiting core beliefs you have identified, you will stimulate the life force inside your body that can facilitate healing of your body and mind. As we think, so we create.

Write out your new, expansive core beliefs here:

____

____

____

____

____

____

____

____

____

____

____

Week 7

As We Think, So We Create

"The mind has great influence over the body and maladies often have their origin there."

Jean Baptiste Moliere

The Law of Attraction

In this universe, there exists a law of attraction that is as real as the law of gravity. It dictates that what we imagine in our minds, we can create in our lives. Our minds are like antennas, transmitting and receiving frequencies of thought. When we fully recognize the power we can wield with our minds, we can learn how to direct it in a positive manner for healing and growth.

When we desire something, we are essentially aligning our minds with the energetic frequency of what we want. When you desire a material object, you think about what it looks like, what color it is, the shape or size, and so forth. Perhaps you desire a specific make and model car. When you think about it, you might imagine what it would feel like to drive it, what color you want it to be, how many doors it has, and so on. After a while, you start expecting it and act as if you will have the exact car of your dreams. When you think in this manner, you are engaging with the law of attraction. You have the desire and the expectation that you will acquire the thing you want. Walt Disney created his successes by working with this law. He believed, "If you dream it, you can do it." Having desire without expectation is ineffective. It is simply a fantasy or wishful thinking that never amounts to anything.

On the other hand, when you combine desire with expectation, your mind becomes a magnet to the good you are calling forth into manifestation. When you align yourself with the principles in the law of attraction, you become a co-creator for the goodness you desire. The greatest challenges are the obstacles that exist in your belief structure. We, as human beings, often hold self-limiting beliefs that we are undeserving of the good we desire or that it is meant for somebody else. We are conditioned to expect very little for ourselves, and so as a result, we put forth very little effort in using our minds to create a better life, a healthier body, and a happier, more joyful heart.

34

10 Steps to Applying the Law of Attraction to Your Health and Well-Being

1. Take control of your thoughts. Shift your focus from what you believe to be wrong to what is right in your health and in your life. Write out what is right with your life here:

____

____

____

____

____

2. Get clear on what you desire for your health. Is it to lose weight, have greater mobility, be allergy free, pain free, addiction free, eliminate food cravings, have more energy, experience a greater sense of well-being in your health and relationships, or be free from depression or anxiety?

____

____

____

____

____

3. Determine what a healthy body would feel like to you. Do you remember a time when you felt your best? What was it like?

____

____

____

____

____

4. Spend a few minutes every day focusing your mind on the image you have created for yourself. The more you focus on the positive you want, the more you will attract the people, opportunities, and support you need to create a healthier you. See it clearly in your mind's eye.

5. Expect to reach your goal. How will that change your life?

____

____

____

____

____

____

6. Give thanks every day for the level of health you are experiencing and any progress you make, no matter how small it is. What you focus on will increase. Write out your heart-felt gratitude here:

____

____

____

____

____

____

____

7. When ideas come to you, take the necessary steps, no matter how small or insignificant they seem. You never know where a step may lead you to next. What ideas have come into your awareness of things you can do or changes you can make to improve your health?

____

____

____

____

____

____

8. Affirm you desired goal as if it has already come into fruition. You need to imagine it is possible to achieve the healing you desire. Complete this sentence. I am so happy and grateful now that I

____

____

____

____

____

9. Surround yourself with people who will support you on your healing journey. Who can you count on in your life to support you on your healing journey?

____

____

____

____

____

10. Release anything in your life that has contributed to the health conditions you want to transform or heal. What are you letting go of that has contributed to your symptoms? This can be thoughts, feelings, memories, old hurts, limiting beliefs, poor self-image, etc.

Week 8

Interconnectedness Between Body, Mind, and Spirit

"The Spirit is life. The mind is the builder. The physical is the result."

Edgar Cayce

Your Energetic Anatomy

Much has been written about the connection between body, mind, and spirit. Years of research into energy medicine have proven there is a direct link between what we think or feel, and the health of our physical body. To truly heal from an illness, one must consider associated thought patterns, beliefs, and emotions that may be connected to the root of the problem. Chronic conditions are a message from the body that the core issue has not yet been resolved. "Incurable" illnesses only mean that the illness cannot be "cured" through outer means alone and we must go within to facilitate true and lasting healing. Different stressors, emotions, and thought patterns will manifest in different parts of the body. If you take the time to listen to your body and be honest with what you think and feel, you will tap into an infinite source of wisdom about yourself. Our bodies are divinely designed to experience the richness of life through all of our senses. They come with a built-in communication system that is also interpreted through our senses.

Our bodies have seven major energy centers with additional secondary centers that connect our physical bodies to our spiritual self through levels of consciousness. Each center, known as a chakra, also corresponds to certain organs and glands in the body along with various emotions and beliefs. The result of an unresolved issue in our consciousness can manifest as a physical imbalance in a specific part of the body. Emotional barriers to love are known to undermine the health of the heart while financial fears tend to create tension and discomfort in the lower back. Digestive problems may reflect unresolved issues around personal power and self-esteem. The list of possible issues is endless and the symptoms they can produce will vary from person to person. What remains consistent are the organs and glands related to specific chakras in the body and the corresponding thought patterns that will migrate to those chakras and have an impact on the physical body.

Here is a brief overview of the seven major chakras, the related physical body parts, the primary functions of each chakra, and some of the issues that will impact the balance of the chakra. If you are struggling with an issue, it can manifest symptomatically in the corresponding physical body part.

39

1.	FIRST CHAKRA

Location: Base of spine.

Physical body parts: Legs, feet, bones, large intestine.

Function: Grounding.

Related issues: Survival, grounding, security, standing up for oneself, connection to the earth.

2.	SECOND CHAKRA

Location: Lower abdomen, sexual organs.

Physical body parts: Sexual organs, lower abdomen, hips, bladder, kidneys.

Function: Desire, pleasure, sexuality, creativity.

Related issues: Money concerns, guilt, sexual problems, urinary problems, ethics in relationships, blocked creativity.

3.	THIRD CHAKRA

Location: Solar Plexus.

Physical body parts: Pancreas, stomach, liver, gall bladder, adrenal glands, spleen.

Function: Personal power, self-esteem.

Related issues: Trust, self-confidence, making decisions, fear, self-esteem, anger and resentment, power struggles.

4.	FOURTH CHAKRA

Location: Center of the chest.

Physical body parts: Lungs, heart, arms and hands, thymus gland, breasts, diaphragm.

Function: Love,

Related issues: Forgiveness and compassion, love, grief, hope, self-centeredness.

5.	FIFTH CHAKRA

Location: The throat.

Physical body parts: Thyroid, parathyroid, esophagus, neck, mouth, jaw, teeth.

Function: Communication, will power and the power of choice.

Related issues: Personal expression, addictions, judgment and criticism.

6.	SIXTH CHAKRA

Location: Center of forehead.

Physical body parts: Eyes, ears, nose, pineal and pituitary glands, brain.

Function: Seeing, intuition.

Related issues: Emotional intelligence, self-evaluation, open to ideas of others.

7.	SEVENTH CHAKRA

Location: Top of the head.

Physical body parts: Central nervous system,

Function: Higher understanding, spirituality, entry point for life force,

Related issues: Faith and inspiration, alienation, depression, sensitivity to light and sound.

What part of your body are you experiencing symptoms in?

____

____

____

____

____

What chakra is connected to the body parts you just wrote down?

____

____

____

____

What is the core issue affecting your body?

____

____

____

____

____

What steps can you take to resolve the underlying issue?

____

____

____

____

____

How do you imagine you would feel after the issue you identified is resolved?

____

____

____

____

____

Week 9

Mirror, Mirror on the Wall

"Our limitations and success will be based, most often, on our own expectations for ourselves. What the mind dwells upon, the body acts upon."

Dennis Waitley

If you want to get insight into some of the limiting beliefs that you may have internalized that are affecting your health and well-being, become aware of how you perceive the world around you. What we perceive outside of ourselves is a reflection of what is going on within our own consciousness. Our world merely reflects back to us what we believe to be true and where we have gotten stuck in the matrix of mass consciousness. We are the ones who give definition and meaning to everything we see. Our bodies mirror back to us what we think and feel about ourselves and how we perceive ourselves in relationship to the world around us. The goal is to become aware of our projections and then evolve the perceptions we have of ourselves and others. It is human nature to project negative qualities onto others until we are willing to own them within ourselves.

Take a few moments and stand in front of mirror. What do you see when you look into your own eyes? What are thoughts that pop into your mind? What image of yourself do you see being reflected back to you? If you find yourself standing in judgment of yourself, not liking what you see, know that you have the power to change your perception. It is not so much changing yourself as it is changing how you see yourself. There are no limits to our perceptions except those we ascribe to out of a conditioned, limited way of seeing. Because of our habitual way of seeing ourselves, we may fail to recognize that the very thing we are trying to avoid looking at holds the key to our healing.

Every health challenge presents the opportunity to transform a part of ourselves into something bigger and better. Our job is to open our hearts and minds to greater possibilities for ourselves than that which we have accepted as our limits up to this point. The meaning of a health issue may not always be clear or obvious in the beginning of your quest for truth, but over time, with some self-reflection, a greater understanding of the thoughts and perceptions underlying a condition will come to the surface for healing. The one necessary pre-requisite is to fully, completely, and unconditionally see yourself with eyes of love right where you are, with whatever your challenges may be. The goal is not to change yourself but rather change the way you perceive yourself.

Look into the mirror again, not to pass judgment, but to recognize the judgment you may hold against yourself. Judgment sabotages our ability to feel whole within ourselves and thus requires healing. Healing comes when there is a change in our perception. When

43

we can see ourselves and others with eyes of love and accept unconditionally what we see with our eyes, we can begin to believe we are good enough right here and right now. That is the beginning of healing the self from within.

Write down the judgments you hold that you are willing to release.

____

____

____

____

Creating a Vision for Health

The first step in creating a vision for optimal health and well-being is to have a clear idea of what that would look like and feel like to you. Begin to create an image in your mind of how a state of optimal health would appear on all levels of your being; physical, mental, emotional, and spiritual. How would you feel? What would be different for you? What is standing in the way of your vision right now?

The second step is believing the vision you have created for yourself is achievable. Having an image alone will not bring you the results you desire. You have to really want it, feel it, emotionalize it, and believe it is possible to manifest it. Emotional energy becomes the fuel of your desire to bring forth your vision into manifestation.

The third step is aligning your thoughts, your actions, your choices, and your daily habits with your image of health for yourself. Write out affirmations, create a vision board, change your eating habits, nourish your heart and mind, develop a spiritual practice, and take time to get out into nature. You cannot achieve a state of health and well-being if the actions you are taking do not support your vision. For example, you cannot continue to eat sugary desserts and lots of pasta and then expect to lose weight. It is not going to happen. Neither can you increase your energy levels if you only eat processed foods that you microwave from a box and sit in front of a TV or computer day and night, never getting any real exercise.

The fourth step is repeating steps one, two, and three, over again until you achieve your desired results. Repetition facilitates change. Our brains do not know the difference between something real and something imagined. By consistently rehearsing in your mind your ideal image for health with all the emotion you can give it, feeling and believing it, you will strengthen your ability to attract to you all that is needed for your vision. It might come in the form of a doctor or healer. It might be a book or cooking class. It could also be a healing modality that is new to you or different type of supplement. The possibilities are endless once you make a decision for health and follow through with the steps you are guided to take.

Perhaps you have a photo of yourself from a time you remember feeling fantastic, when everything was right with your world. That photo of yourself would be great to use with your vision because you have a memory of how you looked and felt at the time the picture was taken. Your body also has a memory of how it felt when all was well. Looking at a photo makes it easier to connect with the felt sense of the vision you are creating in the present. The cells in your body that hold the memory of health will respond to your efforts by releasing stagnant energy that has accumulated over time and begin resonating with your vision of health. Never underestimate the power that lies within the intelligence of your own body. The more you listen to it, honor it, and work with it, the more it will respond to your desires for greater health and well-being.

Write out in detail your vision for greater health and well-being here.

Week 10

Going Within

"No problem can be solved from the level of consciousness that created it."

Albert Einstein

Learn How to Meditate Daily

Meditation is a process of slowing down the mind and body and letting go of all thoughts that may occupy our minds and cause us worry, fear, anger, judgment, or any other negative emotion. Some define it as a state of "emptiness". By letting go, we achieve a state of awareness that gives us both clarity and peace. We can then carry this with us in our daily lives, making our normal experience much more meaningful and mindful. The daily practice of meditation has been proven to have many health benefits. It brings a sense of understanding, compassion, and deeper awareness to people who regularly practice it.

Meditation is not a difficult practice and one can learn the basic techniques fairly quickly. It does take some practice and discipline to integrate it into your daily life, but you do not have to follow a particular religion or have a specific belief to meditate. It is open to all people and all beliefs. Most meditation is done sitting down in a relaxed position. Meditation can be any length, although having at least 15-30 minutes of focused time is ideal. It takes time to quiet the mind and remain in meditation, but there are no rules or time limits as to how you achieve this inner stillness and sense of peace. As you practice meditation you will learn that you can also utilize it "on the go" and in quick moments of stress or indecision.

How to Meditate

Allow 15-30 minutes to practice meditation. Find a quiet location or put on some soft soothing music to help you focus. Quiet is best if possible but use music if it will help. Then, follow these simple steps.

1. Sit or lie somewhere comfortable. Be in a position where you won't fall asleep, but that is comfortable to you and will help you relax.
2. Begin by focusing on your breathing. Focus on the rhythm of the in and out breaths. Practice deep breaths and get a relaxing rhythm going.
3. Focus on relaxing your body and releasing tension in all areas from your head to your toes.
4. Once you are relaxed, try to let go of thoughts and distractions. Don't force them away; just gently focus on them, then let them go in your mind while you focus on your breathing.
5. The goal is to get to a place where you have cleared your mind of all thoughts. Utilize your breathing and focus on the in and out breaths to clear your mind.
6. Clearing your mind is not always easy, so don't get frustrated. Just gently work on this technique. Thoughts may come to your mind during your meditation. Just notice them and then let them go with your next breath.
7. If a thought or feeling comes up regularly, this may indicate there is something you need to work on or clear.
8. You can begin and end the meditation session with a prayer, mantra or an affirmation. Always begin and close your meditation session on a positive note.

Record your daily meditation experience here. Take notice of how you feel, what insights might come to you, perhaps you will see colors or images. There is no right or wrong way to meditate and no two experiences will be alike.

MONDAY

____

____

____

____

TUESDAY

____

____

____

____

WEDNESDAY

THURSDAY

FRIDAY

SATURDAY

SUNDAY

Denials and Affirmations

Our ability to overcome and heal from any affliction is not only possible; it is probable if the laws of healing are engaged. All our happiness, all our health, and all our creativity comes from within us. The source of all transformation originates from within. Our human, intellectual mind wants us to believe that we need something external to change a condition. We become submissive to this belief and accept it, denying our own power. The fact is we have everything we need within us and we can access our internal power with persistent effort. This is really important when you want to bring change to a particular aspect of your health or life experience. The first step is becoming aware we have the power to facilitate healing within ourselves with the proper use of our mind and the second step is actively engaging with that power.

What is a Denial?

A denial is a statement denying something has power over you. It can be a thought, a person, a feeling, or a circumstance in your life. Denials are used to neutralize thoughts of negativity and doubt. A denial doesn't necessarily mean something does not exist. A statement of denial denies that something has power over you, that it is stronger than you, or that it has control over you. You can deny things like fear, pain, old age, or sickness to have any power over you. If your mind was a blackboard and negative self-talk was written all over it, a denial would act as an eraser, wiping away the false beliefs accumulated in this lifetime and clearing the mental space they previously occupied. That is the purpose of using a statement of denial.

Some examples of denial statements are:

- ❖ Nothing or no one can hurt me or make me unhappy.
- ❖ There is nothing to be anxious or fearful about.
- ❖ I cannot inherit sickness.
- ❖ I am not affected by other people's emotions.
- ❖ Pain or sickness has no power over me.
- ❖ My past has no control over me.

Think back over your answers in previous exercises. Pick one thing that has surfaced for you that is adversely affecting your health in some manner. Then, write a denial statement about it here:

____

____

____

____

What is an Affirmation?

An affirmation is a statement that positively asserts the Truth about something, even in the face of evidence to the contrary (Cady 60). You do not need to know how the positive change is going to come about, you just need to believe with faith that the good you desire will manifest for you. There is much power to be released in words of Truth that are spoken with great faith. Affirmations give us strength and align our minds with the Truth of our being. When we align our hearts and minds with Truth and when we desire only good to manifest, the physical body will reflect that Truth back in the form of balance, harmony, health, strength, vitality, and so on.

Some examples of sample affirmations:

- ❖ My thoughts are positive and support my well-being.
- ❖ I am strong, healthy, beautiful, and enjoying my life to the fullest.
- ❖ Everything I do brings me aliveness and growth.
- ❖ I deserve a positive, nurturing environment.
- ❖ I accept myself and love myself unconditionally.
- ❖ I release limiting beliefs and open to new, empowering beliefs.
- ❖ Every cell in my body radiates life, light, and love.

Take the denial statement you wrote out and create a strong affirmation that states the opposite of the problem you are focusing on. Then, take time every day this week to recite the denial and affirmation you wrote until you can easily align your heart and mind with Truth.

____

____

____

____

What do you notice or feel when you recite the denial and affirmation you wrote?

____

____

____

____

Week 11

Master Keys That Open the Pathway to Healing

"If we are willing to do the work, almost anything can be healed."

Dr. Louise Hay

We all have the source of healing and transformation within us. Our bodies are designed to heal and regenerate. It is not a mystical process that only a select few are privileged to access and engage in. Healing is a natural, innate process that dwells within each of us, available to anyone willing to do the necessary work to access it. We just need to learn how. There are some spiritual practices that are keys to accessing and igniting the healing power within. When one engages in these practices, it creates a higher frequency of energy that stirs the life force into action, like the practice of using a tuning fork when tuning a piano. The effectiveness of these key ideas is contingent upon the consistent daily practice and application of each one. You cannot do something for a day or two and expect great results. The following practices need to become as habitual as getting up out of bed in the morning and brushing your teeth. They are the motivating force for change, healing, and personal growth.

MINDFULNESS

Mindfulness is a state of consciousness. It is achieved by turning your focus inward in a more contemplative manner. It is not meant to change anything or respond to situations with an emotional reaction. Rather, mindfulness is an open, more aware state of noticing without judgment what we feel, think, and have going on in the body. It can be a sensation, a constriction, a pain, or a feeling. It involves an acceptance of whatever is happening in the present moment with a heightened sensitivity. You simply still your mind, letting go of all self-judgment and self-criticism, and becoming aware of your own inner wisdom that is just waiting to be discovered. Mindfulness is a reflective state that honors the self and will bring forth much information in the stillness of the mind. It is a way to facilitate change through awareness rather than external effort alone.

First Mindfulness exercise:

First, go to the website www.viacharacter.org and take the strengths survey. After you answer all the questions, print out your results. The top strength for you is your signature strength. This is the strength you use the most in your life. Number 24 is the strength you use the least.

Pick either one of your top strengths or one of your lesser strengths, depending on what you want to work with or strengthen in yourself.

Sit quietly for a few moments and open your mind. Ask yourself how you can consciously use the strength you picked out to improve your health or create positive change in your life. Maybe you need to add humor and take things less seriously. Or perhaps you want to feel more courage and less timid.

Practice using the strength you chose to work with throughout your day.

At the end of your day, write down which strength you focused on and how you used it. Then, write down how using this particular strength made you feel.

____

____

____

____

____

____

____

____

____

Continue using the same strength for a week and then notice what has improved for you. Write down what you noticed.

____

____

____

____

____

____

Second Mindfulness Exercise:

Sit quietly for a few moments and visualize your future self with optimal health, lots of energy, days filled with joy and people around you who love you and support you. Then ask your future self what you need to do to become your future self. Just be still and keep an open mind. Pay attention to the thoughts that come to you.

When you are done, write down all the thoughts and ideas you reflected upon. Choose one and write down the steps you need to take.

Start taking action, one step at a time, and then at the end of the week reflect upon what you did, the progress you made, and how you feel or what has changed for you.

Joy

Another vital key to unlocking the door to healing is found in the energy of joy. Joy is a vibration that uplifts and fuels the cells of the body with vital energy. It is the essence of who you are. We have been programmed to believe that we need to struggle and suffer in order to grow or heal. That is not the truth. You can make a decision to experience joy rather than struggle, regardless of what is going on around you, by changing your belief. It is that simple. You just need to believe you deserve to experience joy in your life. By believing you *deserve* joy you will expand your capacity to open and receive that which brings more joy to your heart.

Other ways to access joy and increase it in your life is to put your energy and focus on the activities that bring you joy. You know what these are by the level of freedom you feel when you engage in them. Joy-filled activities provide you with a greater freedom of expression as they are soul directed rather than personality directed. They are the things you really want to do with your day, the activities that put a spring in your step and a smile on your face versus the things you believe you should be doing.

Learn how to let go of external distractions that deplete your energy and consume your valuable time. You are 100 percent in charge of your time and what you do with it. Your life force is the greatest gift you will ever receive. Take time to look at the areas of your life where you are investing your energy and ask yourself if they bring you joy and energize you or if they deplete you of your vital energy. You cannot heal yourself if you are giving your energy away or participating in activities that deplete you.

Activity to create more joy:

Make a list of ten activities that you love to do, that bring you joy, that you have not done in many months. It can be curling up with a good book, getting a massage or manicure, going to the movies, hiking in the woods, getting together with friends, etc.

____

____

____

____

____

____

____

____

Then write out all the reasons you have had for not doing them.

____

____

____

____

____

____

____

____

____

Pick three of the activities you would love to do right now and create some concrete steps you can take to manifest them in your life.

____

____

____

____

____

____

____

____

____

____

____

Next, mark your calendar with specific dates you are willing to commit to bringing these activities into your life.

After you have completed one of the activities, write down your experience and how much joy you felt by doing it.

____

____

____

____

____

____

____

Try to do this on a consistent basis, varying the activities you choose with the goal of experiencing more joy in your life.

GRATITUDE

Having an attitude of gratitude raises your vibration and cleanses your energetic body. If you are having a bad day or feeling drained, a simple yet powerful way to feel uplifted is to acknowledge the good that exists in your life and give thanks for it. No matter how gloomy things may appear on the surface, there is always something you can find to appreciate and be grateful for. By expressing gratitude, you can lift your spirits and attract more goodness to you.

There is a universal law of increase that states whatever you appreciate and give thanks for will increase in your life. If you want to heal something in your body, instead of just focusing on the problem, give thanks for all the ways your body is serving you well. Appreciate how it digests the food you eat, filters the air you breathe, and moves in any direction you want to go. When you give thanks and express appreciation to your body, the cells in your body receive that information and respond.

Each and every cell has its own awareness and memory of everything you have ever felt and experienced. If you complain about how your body feels or always criticize how it is functioning, it is not going to respond as positively as you would like it to. It is human nature to mentally focus on what hurts or what we believe to be wrong with us. Criticism, judgment, and negativity are lower vibrations and if that is where you are putting all your focus, then that is what you are going to attract more of. Expressing gratitude will take you out of your head, away from thoughts of good or bad, right or wrong, and center you in your heart.

No matter what type of health challenge you may be facing, be it large or small, there is always something positive you can find about your body to appreciate and give thanks for. Gratitude is felt in our hearts. When you give thanks for something, you are opening and expanding your heart. Gratitude not only opens the heart; it also facilitates healing in the body. It is considered a high state of awareness that will magnetize more of what you are thankful for when expressed through the heart center.

Gratitude exercise:

Make a list of all things you appreciate about your body and mind.

____

____

____

____

____

____

____

____

Write down 10 things you appreciate having in your life.

____

____

____

____

____

Write down names of people in your life who you are grateful for.

____

____

____

____

____

Express your appreciation. For yourself, start a gratitude journal. Make a daily list of ten things you are grateful for and read it back to yourself.

For people in your life, you can call them or send them a card expressing your gratitude and appreciation for having them in your life.

Make gratitude a daily practice and notice how things improve in your body and in your life.

NON-VIOLENCE

Non-Violence is an idea and principle to live by. Non-violence can be defined as a reverence for life, not succumbing to pressure from society or others and not over committing oneself, but rather going with what feels right, honoring the way the body is organized, trusting the wisdom contained within, not allowing someone else to dictate what is best for you, and not over-riding the body's own innate process and pace of healing.

Only you can truly know what is best for you, whether it is the right food to eat, the types of exercise to engage in, a spiritual practice that feeds your soul, how you like to be touched, or the best course of treatment for a health condition. You do not need others to agree with or validate your choices to make them right for you. You are the only one who can decide what honors you. Your body communicates with you on a minute to minute basis, letting you know how it feels. To allow someone else to dictate or choose for you the things which you need to choose for yourself gives them authority over you, and that is also considered a form of violence.

Non-violence exercise: Take a few minutes to sit quietly and take your awareness inward. What parts of your body are calling out to you for change? It might be eliminating certain foods, sugar, or alcohol. Perhaps your body wants more exercise or movement. Maybe you need to change some perpetual negative thinking into positive thoughts. It could be your soul calling for a regular spiritual practice. Whatever it is, identify one or more items for each area that doesn't honor or support you and then come up with a better choice that is "non-violent" and more nurturing to your being.

PHYSICAL:

____

____

____

____

____

____

____

____

MENTAL:

____

____

____

____

____

EMOTIONAL:

____

____

____

____

____

____

SPIRITUAL:

____

____

____

____

____

____

____

FORGIVENESS

Forgiveness is an act that plays a key role in healing. Whenever there is sadness, pain, hurt, anger, resentment, guilt, envy, or dis-ease, forgiveness is a necessary part of the healing process. It is almost impossible to heal oneself when there is a burden of blame, shame or lack of forgiveness weighing down the heart. Forgiveness starts in your own heart with yourself for yourself. You cannot truly forgive others if you have not forgiven yourself and released yourself from the bonds of self-judgment. A good place to start is to acknowledge and release the blame we carry in our hearts against ourselves. This cannot be a partial act or part of a conditional agreement you make with yourself. If you with hold forgiveness from yourself you hold yourself hostage to pain and suffering, thereby denying yourself the peaceful healing energies that come with the act of forgiving.

Forgiveness is an inside job. No one else can do it for you. The task is yours alone to complete. It needs to be a wholehearted, unconditional gesture that comes from within. Through the process of forgiveness, one fully accepts and releases all attachments to the past and any grievances that may have been held onto. There is no one correct way to forgive. It is the intention behind the action that is most important.

Forgiveness is not a onetime gesture, either. It is an ongoing process. As long as we continue to judge with our minds, we need to keep forgiving ourselves until we reach the point where we can let go of all judgment and learn how to accept other people and ourselves just as we are. Self-acceptance is the first step in self-forgiveness.

The second step is taking responsibility for everything that you believe has happened to you, thus letting go of all blame. The people and world around you do not cause you suffering. They merely reflect what you believe to be true in your own mind. You are responsible for every thought you think, every word you speak, and every action you take. If you do not like what you feel or see, take responsibility for yourself by changing your perception about yourself, and then observe your new thoughts reflected back to you.

The third and final step in the process of forgiveness is to love oneself totally and unconditionally. You recognize that you are your source of love and you are love. Forgiveness is a gift we give to ourselves to free us from anything we believe has caused us pain. When we choose to forgive, we are choosing life for ourselves. In the process we access the source of healing within ourselves that brings us peace and release from that which is compromising our health and well-being.

Self-forgiveness exercise:

Step 1: Accept yourself unconditionally in this moment as you are.

Step 2: Take responsibility for something you feel has happened to you or caused you pain. Forgive yourself for the part you played.

Step 3: Love and embrace yourself totally and unconditionally until you fully release the pain you are carrying around. You may want to look yourself in the eyes in the mirror and speak words of forgiveness and love to yourself out loud.

Second forgiveness exercise:

Ho'oponopono – A Hawaiian forgiveness ritual - You might want to purchase a wonderful book on this ritual to gain a deeper understanding of the practice. The book is titled Ho'oponopono by Ulrich E. Dupree

Ho'oponopono proceeds from an understanding that we are all connected at some level in consciousness. In this understanding of unity or oneness, nothing can happen in our own world without creating a resonance in the observer. We can only heal problems in the external world when we have addressed the corresponding internal ones. The ritual goes like this:

Step 1: I am sorry ______________________________________

Step 2: Please forgive me ______________________________

Step 3: I love you ______________________________________

Step 4: Thank you ______________________________________

Take each step and repeat the words with the person or problem held in your mind. You can also take each sentence and expand upon it as it relates to your problem, conflict, judgment, condemnation, complaint, or unhappiness. As you intentionally create harmony and peace within yourself, you will be creating harmony and peace in your world. Furthermore, you will heal the wounds that have contributed to your physical problems.

LOVE

"Love Heals All." Love is the creative energy in our universe. There is no energy that vibrates at a higher frequency than pure, unconditional love. Love creates and love heals. Love brings order and harmony. Love is a necessary requirement for maintaining a healthy, vibrant body and mind. Love is a master key for accessing the source of healing within us. Without love, all other efforts are incomplete. I am not speaking about a romantic, emotional kind of love. I am referring to an unconditional state of self-love.

Without self-love we cannot truly love another. We have so many reasons why we do not love ourselves. We look into the mirror and do not always like what we see. We as humans can be quick to pass judgment based upon our perceptions of outer physical appearances. We forget that we are so much more than a physical body. The first step to loving oneself is to accept yourself just as you are in this moment, without exception. There are no buts allowed. To love oneself unconditionally means to be accepting, supporting, honoring, and appreciating the self, right here and right now.

Judgment is a huge obstacle to self-love. Whether you are judging yourself or another person, it ultimately will create a barrier in your ability to love yourself. When we judge another person for any reason, big or small, we are sending a message to our own subconscious that we need to act in a certain way in order to be acceptable and lovable. What happens in our minds is we develop a belief that we will only accept ourselves under certain conditions. Each time we judge another person we are also judging ourselves. This leads to a constant inner dialogue of self-criticism that creates a limiting belief in conditional love for self and others.

To generate more self-love, start with sending love to all parts of yourself. This includes the fearful part, the doubting mind, the critical inner voice, the internal judge, the negative self-talk, and the body image with all its perceived imperfections. Instead of denying their existence, acknowledge their presence within your being and thank them for all the ways they have tried to serve you and protect you. Write a love letter to yourself from your Higher Self, appreciating all your good attributes and the things you do well. You are so much more than a physical body, with many unique qualities. Above all, you are a spiritual being seeking to express your Self through your physical body.

What happens is over time we put up roadblocks because some person or experience left us with a feeling of not being good enough. By sending love to this part of ourselves we can bring healing energy in to transform our limiting beliefs, and as a result, strengthen our overall life force. Our consciousness is multidimensional. It has many facets to its existence. The more love we can send to those parts that we have isolated for one reason or another, the more of our consciousness is brought into alignment with the state of wholeness that exists at the core of our being.

Love has more healing power within its energy than any drug ever will. Our job is to remove the barriers we have erected to loves presence. The supply of love is infinite within us. We hold the master key to accessing it and allowing it to transform us from the inside out.

Exercises for increasing love toward the self and then towards others.

1. Write a love letter to yourself.
2. What would it look like if you were more loving to yourself in the following areas? Make a list of actions step you can take that would increase your self-love.
   a. Physical body
   b. Intimate relationship
   c. Your job/career
   d. Your immediate family
   e. Close friendships

3. Write a powerful affirmation for yourself that affirms more love for yourself. Write your affirmation on several cards and paste them up in several different places so you can constantly see it during your waking hours.

4. In the morning, spend 10-15 minutes in silent meditation, visualizing yourself as a beacon of love. See this love fill your heart up until it is full. Imagine your heart is like the sun and then see your love flowing out in rays of light from your heart to those around you during your day.

5. Find a picture of yourself when you were a child and talk to that younger self about giving and receiving unconditional love from you.

6. Choose a physical challenge or pain you are experiencing. Sit with that physical problem and ask it where did it come from? What is the message it is trying to communicate to you? What does it need to heal? Then, thank this part of your body for helping you heal. See it in balance and in a state of health. Affirm to this part of your body the steps you will take to facilitate healing. Perhaps there are some thoughts or emotions that need to be addressed. Send love to this part of your body while you are affirming health and healing for it.

____

____

____

____

____

____

____

____

____

____

____

Week 12

The Healing Path

"Every health challenge presents the opportunity to transform a part of ourselves into something bigger and better."

Live as a Spiritual Being Having a Human Experience

Our deepest fear is not that we are inadequate. Our deepest fear is that we are powerful beyond measure. It is our light, not our darkness that most frightens us. We ask ourselves, who am I to be brilliant, gorgeous, talented, fabulous?

Actually, who are you not to be?

You are a child of God. Your playing small does not serve the world. There is nothing enlightened about shrinking so that other people won't feel insecure around you. We are all meant to shine, as children do. We were born to manifest the glory of God that is within us. It is not just in some of us; it is in everyone. And as we let our own light shine, we unconsciously give other people permission to do the same. As we are liberated from our own fear, our presence automatically liberates others.

Excerpt from <u>A Return to Love: Reflections on the Principles of a Course in Miracles</u> by Marianne Williamson

What if your soul could speak to you like a close dear friend? What do you think it would say to you?

____

____

____

____

____

____

____

____

____

The health of our physical body is inseparable from our core beliefs about ourselves and the lives we live. We have become conditioned to believe that our physical body is something that needs to be managed and treated as a disease process. What really needs to be managed is our mind. Our bodies may be vulnerable to infections, injuries, and illnesses, but they are not the cause of our afflictions; and we are not powerless victims of a disease process.

I invite you to expand your perception of who you are and what is possible in the realm of healing. You have a physical body that needs proper care and nourishment to perform necessary daily functions. You also have an energetic body that inhabits your physical body. This is made up of your emotions and thoughts that are moving in and through your conscious mind, and beliefs that are active in your subconscious mind. Every thought you think and every emotion you experience activates a physiological response within your body. Cleanse your body and mind from everything that is not life giving.

Challenge yourself to expand and transform your existing belief structure to support a greater perspective of what is possible for you and your life. Trust that everything that happens is meant to help move you into a greater version of yourself. Make every word, every feeling, and every thought align with the highest vision of health possible for you. Learn how to engage the power of your mind to create health and well-being. Bring more joy into days. Take time to meditate. And remember, the body has the capacity to heal from almost anything when given the right support. Live as a spiritual being having a human experience!

Visualize with a New Set of Eyes

Decide what you really want to feel in your body. What do you desire for your health and well-being? Using your imagination, create a clear vision of what that is. Write your vision out in detail here:

____

____

____

____

____

____

____

Next, use your imagination to see yourself as already having what you desire for your greater health and well-being. What does it look like? What would change for you if you felt and looked this way? How is your life better by achieving this health goal? Write it all out here:

____

____

____

____

____

____

____

Bring your emotions into your visualization process. Imagine what it would feel like to accomplish your health and wellness goals? Spend a few minutes every day holding the image you have clearly defined in your mind. Practice putting your mind in harmony with the good you desire for yourself. Imagine what it will feel like to have more energy or a stronger digestion or perhaps a pain free body. Whatever your goal, believe that it is achievable.

The fourth and final step is to be open and receptive to the guidance you will receive. Learn to listen to your still small voice inside. Become aware of the subtle messages coming from your body through symptoms and sensations.

We are conditioned to always focus on what is wrong with us, what needs to be "fixed" or "cured." I am asking you to shift your focus to an image of yourself having already received the healing you desire or the change in your health condition that brings you a greater feeling of ease and well-being. Energy follows thought, so every time you focus on the good, you are using your mind like a magnet to attract greater good to you. If you want healing, by focusing on the end result you want, you are magnetizing with your mind that which best would serve you in achieving the results you desire.

Write down your thoughts here as you practice visualizing yourself receiving the healing you desire throughout the week.

Key Concepts to Remember

- ❖ Symptoms are the universal language of our body and soul, presenting us with information to which we were previously unconscious.
- ❖ If you just attend to the physical aspect, you may change the presentation of the original symptom, but you will not have true and lasting healing.
- ❖ By the time we have manifested a symptom, some form of stress has already had an impact on our ability to internally maintain balance and alignment of body, mind, and spirit.
- ❖ Due to the multidimensionality of our being, our physical bodies often reflect what is going on within other levels of our consciousness.
- ❖ Curing is a passive state. Healing is more than eliminating symptoms. It is restoring the whole person to a state of optimal health and well-being.
- ❖ The image you hold of yourself will either promote your health and well-being or compromise it.
- ❖ You open the doorway to healing when you can view a malady you suffer from as a stepping stone rather than a stumbling block.
- ❖ Suffering is a reminder that there is a conflict between the human self and the spiritual self.
- ❖ Every emotion has a corresponding response system in the brain that causes a physiological response in the body.
- ❖ Beliefs are formed in our minds based upon our perceptions of the world around us.
- ❖ Expansive core beliefs affirm the truth of who we are.
- ❖ Limiting core beliefs are rooted in misconceptions we hold about ourselves and the world around us.
- ❖ What we imagine in our minds we can create in our lives.
- ❖ The goal is not to change yourself but rather to change how you perceive yourself.
- ❖ Wholeness is an idea. It implies a state of balance between our physical, mental, emotional, and spiritual selves.
- ❖ By consistently rehearsing in your mind your ideal image for health with all the emotion you can give it, feeling and believing it, you will strengthen your ability to attract to you all that is needed for your vision.
- ❖ Never underestimate the power that lies within the intelligence of your own body.
- ❖ Denial statements cleanse the mind just as a detox cleanses the body.

- ❖ Affirmations give us strength and align our minds with the real truth of our being.
- ❖ Self-acceptance is the first step in self-forgiveness.
- ❖ Healing is a natural innate process that dwells within each of us, available to anyone willing to do the necessary work to access it.
- ❖ Your biography becomes your biology.
- ❖ Personal power is necessary to sustain health and wellness.
- ❖ Chronic conditions are messages from the body that a core issue has not been resolved.
- ❖ Suppressing symptoms is like putting the body on mute.

About the Author

Mauree has been a healing presence in other people's lives for over 30 years. She is a Functional Medicine Certified Health Coach, an Integrative Nutrition Certified Health Coach, a Certified Bioenergetic Practitioner, a Certified Massage Therapist, a Reiki Master, and the author of the book: <u>Cracking Your Body's Code</u>. She is also certified by the American Association of Drugless Practitioners.

She established the Center for Holistic Healing Arts for people who wanted to pursue safe, holistic, alternative healing strategies and needed a place to receive the support and guidance they were looking for. Mauree also offers customized individual and group coaching in person and virtually. Her life is dedicated to educating and empowering individuals to take control of their health and improve the quality of their lives.

For more information or to contact the author, visit the website at:
www.MaureeKai.com